Miss Violet's Doll's House

Magical makes for your miniature world

Sam McKechnie

PAVILION

COME IN
Miss Violet's doll's house 6
Tiny tales to big ideas 7
Playing with scale 8
Tools and materials 10

HELLO MISS VIOLET
- Miss Violet, ma cherie 14
- Miss Violet's haute couture 16
- Singing in the rain 24

MOVING IN
- Home sweet home 30
- Naming your house 34

KITCHEN
- You'll always find her in the
  kitchen at parties 38
- *Sur la table* 40
- Food, glorious food 44
- A clean sweep 48
- Miss Violet in the kitchen 52
- Prettiest of tables 54
- Bobbin stool 58
- Tea party garland 62
- Miss Violet's Tea Party 66

PARLOUR
- Make yourself comfortable 70
- Mirror, mirror on the wall 72
- From the chandeliers 76
- Candlelit mirrors 80
- Parlour games a plenty 84
- Love letters 86
- Fire! Fire! 90
- 'Tis the season to be jolly 94
- Miss Violet's Christmas 98

BOUDOIR AND EN SUITE

- A place where dreams are made 102
- Pressed flower wallpaper 104
- The nights are drawing in 108
- Bath time 112
- Magic carpets 114
- Top drawers 118
- Fairytale dreaming 122
- Golden slumbers 124
- Sweet dreams Miss Vi 128

GARDEN

- Come into the garden 132
- Wait a minute Mr Postman 134
- Clothes line 138
- Laundry day is a family
  affair 142
- Garden pond 144
- Instant garden 148
- Strawberries and dreams 152
- Magic star garland 156
- Beautiful creatures 160
- Miss Violet's Midsummer's Eve 164

MISS VIOLET'S GUIDE
TO STYLISH LIVING

- *La vie of Miss Vi* 167
- Kitchen 168
- Christmas 169
- Parlour 170
- Boudoir and bedroom 171
- *Les fleurs* (flowers for walls
  and floors) 172
- Valentines and violets 173
- Friends and creatures 174
- House signs and flowers 175
- Rose Red's perfect looking
  glass 176
- Fabrics for walls and floors 177
- Roses and cats 184

RESOURCES 186
THANK YOU 188
ABOUT US 190

COME IN

MISS VIOLET'S DOLL'S HOUSE

I have been fascinated by doll's houses since
childhood. By writing this book, I wanted to be
able to show others how to create a simple miniature
world. Building a home from boxes can be equally
as satisfying as being given a glamorous ready-made
house, so do not be put off by budget or skill. This
book aims to help you see the beauty in the mundane,
opening your eyes, say, to a fallen piece of foil upon
the ground - *voilà* - a mirror for your doll's house!
A bobbin? A stool for your doll's table! Bottle caps
make wonderful dishes... I could go on and on...

Oh, to have a little
  house,
To own the hearth
  and stool and all.

TINY TALES to BIG IDEAS

I've always been an avid reader, and some of my favourite
authors, from childhood still to this very day, have
been inspired by the miniature. Beatrix Potter flooded
my imagination; even now when very tired, I often exclaim
that 'I am worn to a raveling' (*The Tailor of Gloucester*).
For me, bumblebees will always be Babbitty Bumbles.

Another firm favourite is *Miss Happiness and Miss Flower*
by Rumer Godden, and the wonderful *The Diddakoi*, and I
cannot forget the excitement conjured up by the beguiling
imagination of Mary Norton, the creator of *The Borrowers*.
I still believe that they might be living under my
floorboards. Now, there's a thought...

PLAYING with SCALE

I am drawn to the theatrical and unexpected,
so giant roses on my walls and a simply enormous
strawberry for lunch makes perfect sense to me
and Vi. We may have big chairs and little tables
and fried eggs that make no sense at all, but
our house has a character all of its own.

Miss Violet's home became a mixture of vintage
furniture, handmade pieces and antique scraps.
The scraps used throughout this book are from
my own collection and are a treasure trove of
furniture, fripperies and fancies. I have found
these over the years on screens, in albums and
on Victorian Valentines. These are also known
as lithographs, which date back to the early
19th century. Victorian ladies and gents would
paste their chosen scraps into albums and
make keepsakes, Valentine's cards and tokens.
Miss Violet is rather taken with this tradition.

Whilst detail is important, Miss Violet would
not want you to worry about perfection. In fact
imperfections can change the everyday into the
unique. Using old drawers, cupboards or shoe boxes
is a wonderful way to build a house room by room
(in fact, some of the world's oldest doll's houses
have been built this way). If you already have a
ready-made doll's house, that's fantastic, but if
you don't, don't fret.

TOOLS and MATERIALS

You will probably have most of the tools listed below
but if not, most are easily found. Your local art
shop will have a lot of useful equipment. I would
definitely recommend investing in a flower press as
pressing flowers is such a lovely pastime anyway -
most toy shops or online auctions sell inexpensive
ones. Here's my essential kit...

1. Clear tape
2. Eraser (polar bear optional)
3. Drawing pins
4. Thread (various colours)
5. Hole punch
6. Scissors and wire cutters
7. Poster tack (you can use
   the traditional blue version
   as shown opposite, but
   the white variety is
   particularly useful)
8. Pins
9. Glue stick
10. Washi tape (pandas optional)
11. Paperclips
12. Needles
13. Pliers
14. Pen
15. Pencil and crayon
16. Wire (20 gauge)
17. Flower press
18. Cotton wool
19. Single hole punch
20. Hot-melt glue gun

Water-based glue will also be very useful as we
continue through the book. For painting makes,
I recommend acrylic or gouache paint - both are
water-based but acrylic glazes will add a little
extra shine to your décor.

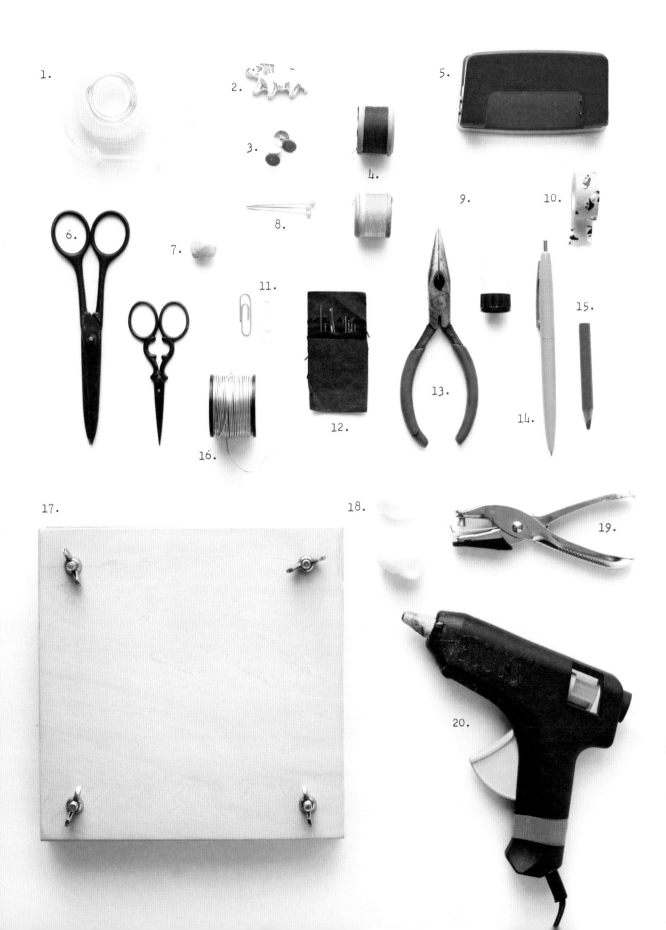

1.

2.

3.

4.

5.

6.

7.

8.

9.

10.

11.

12.

13.

14.

15.

16.

17.

18.

19.

20.

HELLO MISS VIOLET

Miss Violet, ma cherie

Violet and I became inextricably entwined in 2016 before my first visit to Japan. As a rosy-cheeked, disco dancing, sometimes shy woman, I needed a friend to travel with me, and as budgets didn't quite stretch, Violet - my fashionista brave alter ego - jumped right in.

As I travelled across Japan to run doll-making workshops in high-fashion stores, as an ice-breaking greeting, transcending the difficulty of lostness in translation, each customer I met became an echo of Miss Vi. I drew hundreds of the ladies I met, from city to city - some with giant roses on their heads, some with side buns, some with glasses and fringes - and all with rosy cheeks. Violet was my constant companion under the *sakura* and into many feasts. *Kan pai!*

Back home in Battersea, Violet had taken on a life of her own and murmurings had been murmured across London Town, and these many murmurings were wondering who exactly was this darling girl? Where did she come from? And did her fabulous *je ne sais quoi* extend to her home? Was there perhaps someone to tell us? Fortunately for all of us, there is.

Welcome to the world of Miss Violet.

OUR MUSE
Every doll's house needs its muse and I have included a very familiar one especially for you - simply turn to the back of the book and pop her out. Conveniently for Violet, you'll also find her ready-to-wear capsule wardrobe there too (plus extra style inspiration on the following pages).

I hope this paper doll will inspire you to create or search markets and charity shops for some friends for Miss Vi. Whether it's Lady Tulip, Mrs Homily, Ms Rabbit or Duchess Marigold, whoever turns up at the door of Miss Violet's house will always be welcome.

Miss Violet's Haute Couture

Here are some select pieces from Violet's
covetable closet. Photocopy the outfits
or download them via the link on page 167,
then cut them out and attach to your paper
doll with a little poster tack to keep
Miss Vi in style. You could even create
your own collection - Vi prides herself
on finding up-and-coming designers.

BALL GOWN

EARRINGS

CHARM NECKLACE

GLAMOROUS SHOES

SIMPLE DAY
DRESSES

FAIRY DRESS AND
USEFUL WAND

WITCH DRESS

OPTIONAL
TRANSPORT

NICE
ROSE
HAT

DAY
DRESSES

17

RUN AWAY
TO JOIN
THE CIRCUS
OR BE A
SHOW GIRL

BEE BOPPERS

DENIM
PINAFORE

RAINBOW
SOCKS

18

DAISY HAT

MAGIC PIERROT
DRESS

LITTLE RED
RIDING HOOD
OUTFIT

BASKET AND DOG

BASKET AND
BAGUETTE

POSY FOR
GRANDMA

19

EVENING CAPE

POSH DRESS

FAUX FUR STOLE

MACKINTOSH

MAGPIE GOWN

WELLINGTON BOOTS

20

DAY
COAT

BRIDE

HOT
WATER
BOTTLE

VIOLET
BOUQUET

HAIR BOWS

POSH COAT

NIGHT
DRESS

LOVE LETTER

HIPPY
LEGS

SLEEPING
VIOLET FACE

BUNNY SLIPPERS

21

UMBRELLA (BROLLY)

RAINBOW DRESS

CHRISTMAS

SPARE HANGERS

22

CANDY
CANE
DRESS

SUFFRAGETTE
DRESS

COMFY
DRESS

Singing in the Rain

RAINDROPS ON NOSES

- scraps (see pages 166-185)
- scissors
- glue stick
- cocktail umbrella

SINGING IN THE RAIN

Vi and I have always loved a
cocktail and now we have the perfect
excuse to indulge. I love foil
umbrellas but the paper ones look
just as beautiful and create a
showstopping effect.

1. Simply select your scraps and
   cut them out.

2. Using a little glue, stick the
   scraps onto the upside of your
   paper or foil umbrella.

sunshine and showers

MOVING IN

HOME SWEET HOME

'There's no place like home.'

[L. Frank Baum, *The Wizard of Oz*]

Home is where the heart is, and no one knows this quite
like Miss Violet. It's simple to begin your own doll's
house - just think small and beautiful and you're well on
your way to creating your miniature house.

Make your own floral wallpaper, mix and match fabrics, or
plant a thimble garden - find your own finishing touches
that add that *je ne sais quoi*.

Where better to host a fabulous soirée, drink tea or write
a love letter than the comfort of your own doll's house?
So put on your ruby slippers, click your heels three times
and let's begin...

Bits and bobs
- a box, drawer or doll's house
- a good removal firm (your hands)
- a selection of doll's house
  furniture
- a small creature (everyone needs
  the company of a pet)
- scraps (see pages 166-185 for
  paper furnishings such as rugs,
  chairs and flowers)

If using a cardboard box, you may want
to cut out a window, depending on the
view outside.

NAMING YOUR HOUSE

Have you ever wanted to live somewhere else?
Perhaps a little house with flowers around
the door and a thatched roof - Rose Cottage.
What about an Art Deco apartment looking
out over the city - Lucretia Heights?
A Georgian farmhouse - Snooty Manor. A two-up
two-down in a little town - 3 Hope Street?
Here's the chance to create your dream home,
village or town. The sky's the limit.

Miss Violet and I have kept it simple.

Bits and bobs
- card
- scrap of your choice (see pages 166-185)
- letter transfers or pen

And name away...

KITCHEN

You'll Always Find Her in the Kitchen at Parties

Is there anywhere in the home quite so comforting as a cosy kitchen?

The warmth, the fire crackling, oven cooking, kettle whistling, potatoes steaming, bacon sizzling, lemons zesting, coffee brewing, cakes baking, eggs frying, peas boiling...

The kitchen has always been my favourite room of the house and Miss Violet's is the cat's pyjamas.

You'll always find her in the kitchen at parties - whilst by far the cosiest of corners, it's also where the most fun can be had. A place for tears to be shed, secrets shared, ice cream scooped, or a large, lonely gin supped.

So no matter how you make it, your kitchen will be the heart of your doll's home.

Sur la Table

TEA IS ON THE TABLE

- scissors
- card
- acrylic or gouache paint (in any colour)
- paint brush
- scraps (see pages 166-185)
- glue stick
- water-based varnish
- 2 cotton reels (bobbins)
- hot-melt glue gun

SUR LA TABLE

For me the kitchen is the heart of the home, and a
great kitchen table is a must for your doll's house.
I have created Miss Violet's table by using empty
wooden bobbins and some card. Vintage bobbins can be
easily found in charity shops, markets or online
auctions but you could always buy these new. Whilst
they look rather beautiful with their thread left
on, for this make I have used two empty wooden
reels. Bobbin tables can also be made for other
rooms of the house.

1. Cut out a circle of card (be sure to make this
   larger than the end of your bobbin) and paint the
   card in your chosen colour. Leave to dry.

2. Cut out your scraps and, using a glue
   stick, glue these on to your table top (as
   pictured).

3. When dry, finish your table top with a coating
   of water-based varnish.

4. Paint the sides of your bobbins in your chosen
   colour (here I have used acrylic paint).

5. Once dry, glue your bobbins on top of each other
   with a hot-melt glue gun.

6. Finally, glue the table top onto the stacked
   bobbins - *prêt à manger*.

tea's ready!

Food, Glorious Food

FROM THE TINIEST TART TO THE
SMALLEST SAUSAGE

- oven
- 140g/5oz oven-bake modelling clay
- blunt knife
- pin
- pen lid (for pastry tart-cutting)
- baking tray
- acrylic paints (use as many
  colours as you can find)
- fine paint brush

FOOD, GLORIOUS FOOD

Doll's house food is extraordinary and no one appreciates this more than Miss Vi, who loves a sausage, egg and chips supper, one of her famous Queen of Hearts jam tarts and a cheeky glass of wine for good measure.

1. Preheat the oven to 110°C/225°F/Gas $\frac{1}{2}$, then gently knead your clay until it starts to soften. Next, decide what's for dinner!

2. To make peas or beans, roll out tiny balls of clay, only slightly larger than a pinhead, and stick them together into a little pile.

3. For chips or fries, cut out a small square of clay with a blunt knife, then slice lines across the top to mark each individual one. Pile up the chips into a stacked portion - they will bond together during the baking process.

4. For fried eggs, roll out two balls of clay for each egg, one smaller than the other, then squash them gently with the tip of your finger. Pop the small pieces in the centre of the larger pieces and you'll be sunny-side up!

5. To make sausages, take a little clay and roll it between your finger and thumb until you have the perfect sausage shape.

6. Miss Violet needs her 5-a-day as much as the next doll. Bananas can be rolled out in the same way as sausages. Once rolled, simply pinch one end to create a stalk. For apples, roll little balls of clay, adding little stalk indentations with a pin.

7. To avoid tarts with soggy bottoms, thinly roll out a small ball of clay. Using the base of your pen lid as a mini pastry cutter, press the bottom of the lid into the clay to cut out a perfect circle - one for each tart. Using the tip of the pen lid, make an indentation in the centre of each one (to hold your painted filling).

8. Transfer everything to the baking tray and bake for 30 minutes; then remove the tray from the oven and leave to cool.

9. When your food is stone cold, start painting. I used bright green for the peas (you could use orange paint to make baked beans), a golden yellow for the chips with a dollop of red for ketchup, white for the fried eggs with a sunny yellow yolk and a mix of browns for well-cooked sausages. Violet prefers a ripe banana, so I added spots of brown to the yellow base coat. For a showstopping finish, leave an unpainted heart shape in the centre of the red tart filling. Allow the paint to dry for a least one hour. *Bon appétit!*

A Clean Sweep

A BROOM IS FOR LIFE, NOT JUST
FOR HALLOWEEN

- 2 colourful spools of
  cotton thread
- scissors (witch optional)
- 1 twig, approximately 5cm/2in
  in length
- handful of hay or dried
  herbs (fennel is particularly
  good for dust-busting)

A CLEAN SWEEP

One thing Violet insists upon, that's essential for good housekeeping,
is a solid broom. It clears out the cobwebs and sweeps away the dust.
You might like to help Violet give her stylish abode a good spring
clean. On second thoughts, she's perfectly capable of handling her broom.

1. Choose two contrasting coloured threads to match the colour scheme
   of your kitchen. Here I have used green and mauve to create block
   stripes of colour.

2. For each thread cut a length approximately 50cm/20in long, then
   double them up to create two thicker 25cm/10in lengths.

3. Using the twig as your broom handle, gather a small bundle of
   hay or dried herbs around the base of the twig.

4. Secure the bundle to your broom, about 2.5cm/1in from the
   base of the handle, by tightly winding the length of one of
   the threads around the top of the bristles. Knot and trim the
   excess thread to secure, then repeat with the remaining
   thread, winding the contrasting colour above the first to
   create a striped effect.

5. Once the bristles of your broom are firmly in place, carefully
   trim away any unruly strands of hay or herbs with a pair of
   scissors and *voilà*! Your broom is ready to use. Cobwebs be gone!

MISS VIOLET IN THE KITCHEN

It's the day for an excursion
and Miss Violet is off to visit
her Grandmama. The cat has got
the cream and Violet has her
pretty hat and little red cape.
Be careful not to stray from the
path, Miss Vi. À bientôt.

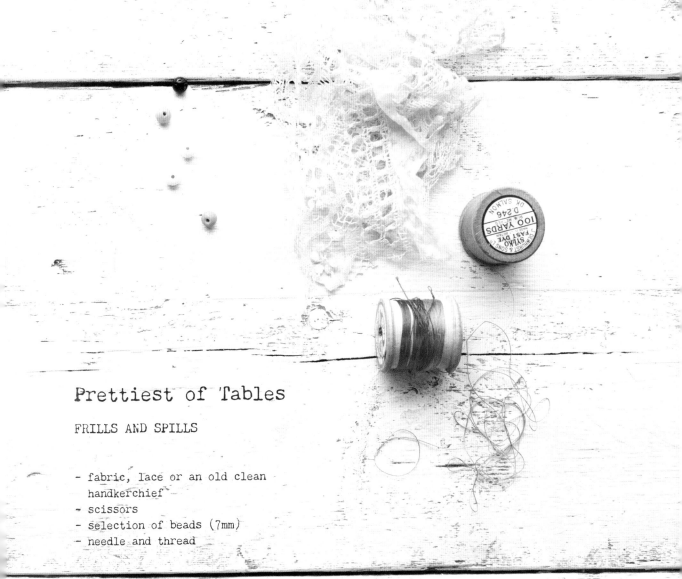

Prettiest of Tables

FRILLS AND SPILLS

- fabric, lace or an old clean
  handkerchief
- scissors
- selection of beads (7mm)
- needle and thread

PRETTIEST OF TABLES

It's time to lay a table fit for a queen as Miss
Violet's friends are popping by for a cosy kitchen
supper. Don't forget the salt and the jam tarts.
A tablecloth is also a must in a well-dressed home.

As a country girl, Miss Vi is inspired by traditional
milk jug covers, with sewn glass beads to weigh
down the corners. Essential for every milkmaid.

1. Cut a circle of fabric a little larger
   than your table top. Finer fabrics work
   best for this make and whilst I have
   used a vintage floral cotton, lace or
   an old clean handkerchief would also
   look pretty.

2. Gather some beads (here I have used
   Indian glass ones from a bead shop).

3. Thread a needle with your chosen thread
   and sew a running stitch around the edges
   of the table cloth, adding a bead every
   three stitches. (To add a bead, simply
   thread one onto your needle and secure
   it in place with a stitch.)

4. When you've finished decorating the fabric
   with beads, secure your running stitch
   with a final knot. When you place the
   cloth on the table the beads should hang
   down over the edge.

Bobbin Stool

PULL UP A CHAIR AND
REST YOUR PINS

- cotton reels (bobbins)
- acrylic or gouache paint
  (in your chosen colours)
- paint brush
- scissors
- scraps (see pages 166-185)
- glue stick
- water-based varnish
- fabric
- cotton wool balls
- needle and thread
- hot-melt glue gun

BOBBIN STOOL

'Pull up a chair, sit down for a while
and tell me all about it', said Vi

Over tea, the friends chatted well into the night, and put
the world to rights. Pull up a chair... or rather, take
a pew. These stools are easy-peasy and so much fun to make.
I have used empty vintage wooden cotton reels here as I
wanted to paint them myself, but you could also use new
reels. Ones with the thread on would look rather lovely
too. This make is very versatile and could also be used
for a foot stool, bedside table (without the cushion) or
a coffee table.

1. Paint a bobbin in your chosen colour (I use acrylic or
   gouache paint).

2. Cut out some scraps.

3. Once the paint on the bobbin is dry, glue the scraps
   onto the side with a glue stick.

4. Apply a layer of varnish and leave to dry.

5. Take a piece of fabric and a cotton wool ball.

6. Pop the cotton wool ball on the underside of the fabric
   and draw a rough circle around the ball, allowing at
   least 1cm/½in extra for the hem, then cut out the
   marked circle.

7. Sew a running stitch around the edge of the fabric,
   holding the cotton wool ball inside as you go. Pull
   your thread to gather the stitches and knot to enclose
   the cotton wool inside the fabric.

8. With your hot-melt glue gun, put a dot of glue on the
   top of the bobbin, and stick your cushion on top.

Tea Party Garland

FORGET ME NOT

- seasonal flowers (here I've used
  a selection of pansies, violas,
  forget-me-nots and leaves)
- flower press or heavy book
- thread
- scissors
- glue stick or water-based glue

TEA PARTY GARLAND

Oh how I love these dainty garlands
and would give anything to be tiny
under these giant pressed flowers.
I wanted to create a special garland
for Violet's tea party and I think her
guests will be rather impressed. A tea
party with friends is always an event
at Miss Violet's house: the piano tuned,
jam tarts baked, cakes adorned. With
instruments at the ready, and pop to
be popped, Miss Vi and her friends can
enjoy themselves under a sky of flowers,
until the sun goes down.

1. Pick some small seasonal flowers.

2. Using a flower press or heavy book, press
   them carefully.

3. Leave to dry for 1 week.

4. After a week, carefully remove from the
   press or book.

5. Measure out some thread to your required
   length (I used 25cm/10in).

6. Dab a little glue on the reverse of a
   flower in its centre and press down on
   to the thread.

7. Continue to add flowers along the thread.

8. Once finished, leave to dry for 10 minutes
   or so, then hang.

'Nothing quite
like a sing-
song at the
doll's house'

PARLOUR

Make Yourself Comfortable

The Queen was in the parlour and this is
exactly where Miss Violet likes to enjoy
her bread and honey - with a cup of tea for
good measure.

A doll's life is delightful yet demanding,
and where better for our Vi to rest her
weary pins than the comfort of a chic,
homemade parlour?

This room has many names - salon, sitting
room, drawing room and living room to name
but a few. Whichever you use, it's easy to
create a miniature piece of heaven with your
own fair hand. Head for your own bohemia and
pull out some favourite fabrics.

A parlour, Violet feels, should always have
a drinks trolley. Anyone for a gin and tonic?

it's a doll's life

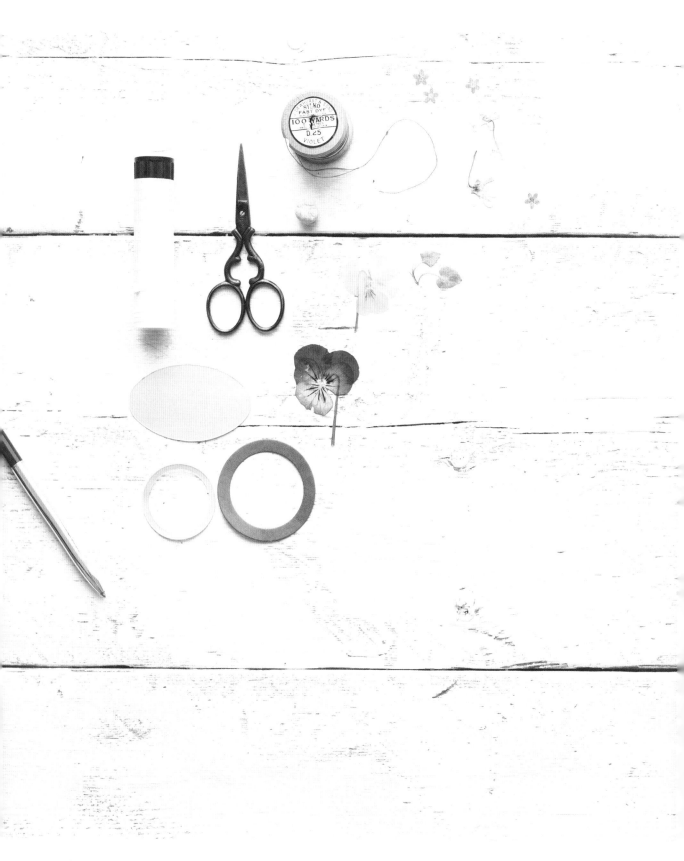

Mirror, Mirror
on the Wall

VIOLET IS THE FAIREST
OF THEM ALL

- card
- scissors
- kitchen foil
- glue stick
- thread
- washi tape
- pens
- pressed seasonal flowers

MIRROR, MIRROR ON THE WALL

Some of the loveliest finds adorning Violet's
walls are old game counters, stamps and scraps,
and this make shows how to create a few more.
Portraits, mirrors and landscapes can all be
designed this way, and make beautiful features
for your walls. Art should be a moveable feast
for the eyes, so here are some of Violet's
finest ideas to furnish your miniature home.

1. To make a mirror, cut out your shape from
   some card, and smooth a small piece of
   kitchen foil over the top. If you wish
   to add a frame, cut a oval-shaped ring
   from your card and glue over the edges
   (as pictured on the previous page). To
   hang your mirror, add a loop of thread
   and fix to the back of the mirror with a
   small strip of washi tape.

2. I like ovals for portraits, and here
   I have drawn some ladies who, Violet
   assures me, were her great aunts. For
   dried flower pictures, simply cut a shape
   out of card and glue a pressed flower
   on top. As with the mirror, it's easy
   to add a frame and hang on your wall.

3. Keep your eyes open for old stamps,
   cards, game pieces and labels to add
   to your doll's house art collection.

TWIST

LOOP
AND
TWIST

A

C

B

BEND

BEND

- Thread wire A through loop B
- Thread loop C over wire A

From the Chandeliers

LIVE LIKE A LADY

- pliers or strong scissors
- aluminium wire (20 gauge)
- ruler
- glass beads (7mm)
- sequins
- hot-melt glue gun
- acrylic paint
  (white, yellow, orange)
- paint brush

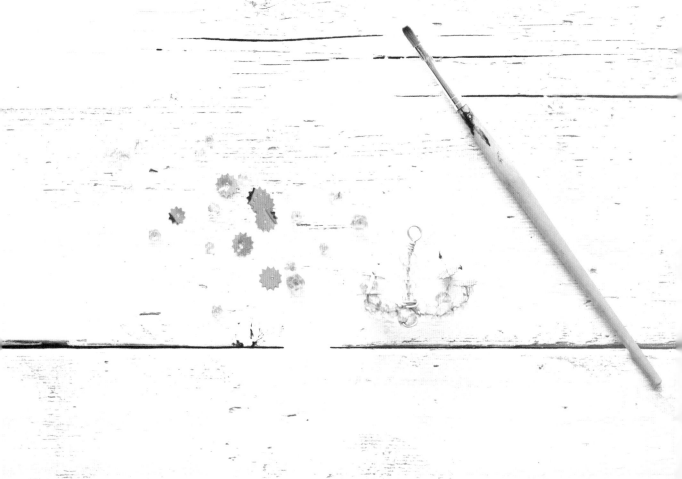

FROM THE CHANDELIERS

Where there's a palace, there's a chandelier. Marie-Antoinette was quite fond of them and Miss Violet is rather partial too. Aside from adding grandeur, sparkle and gravitas, chandeliers are also terribly useful for hanging paper chains and tinsel at Christmas time. Frivolous and functional.

1. Use the guide on page 76 to help you build your chandelier. Using pliers or strong scissors, cut a piece of wire to approximately 10cm/4in. Be sure to leave a straight piece approximately 5cm/2in, then bend the bottom half of the wire into a 'U' shape. This will make your first arm.

2. For your second arm, cut a piece of wire to 15cm/6in. Twist the wire in the centre to make a loop and thread your first arm through the loop.

3. Cut a final piece of wire to 13cm/5in and bend a loop on the end. Thread this on to the first arm as well and tighten all four pieces into a twist using the pliers.

4. Bend each of the four arms up towards the sky. Thread the arms with beads, leaving a gap of 1cm/$\frac{1}{2}$in at the top of each arm. End each bead row with a sequin, and secure in place with a dab of hot-melt glue.

5. Once all four arms are adorned with beads and topped with sequins, thread the central stem with beads, leaving 1cm/$\frac{1}{2}$in at the top. Now twist this into a loop to hang from the ceiling.

6. Cover the ends of each arm generously with some thick white acrylic paint. Leave until dry, then finish with a little yellow and orange paint for the flames.

Candlelit Mirrors

FLICKERING CANDLE LIGHT

- card
- scissors
- kitchen foil
- glue stick
- aluminium wire (20 gauge)
- strong scissors
- pliers
- washi tape
- acrylic paint (white, orange,
  yellow, brown; gold optional)
- paint brush
- beads (5mm, 6mm and 7mm)
- sequins
- hot-melt glue gun

CANDLELIT MIRRORS

Bring a little old-fashioned chic to your parlour.
A *girondelle* is simply a mirror with candle holders
attached that help reflect candle light back into the
room. So add a little extra clarity to Miss Vi and
her friends by making a pair of bespoke candlelit
mirrors. Terribly glamorous and just that little
bit French, *n'est-ce pas?*

1. Cut out a card shape for your mirror, then cut
   out a small piece of foil that is slightly smaller
   than the card base. Smooth the foil a little and
   use a glue stick to secure it in place in the
   centre of the card, leaving a small border of card
   around the edges of the foil so you can create a
   frame for your mirror later.

2. Take approximately 18cm/7in of wire and, using
   your pliers, twist (as pictured on the previous
   page) to make two prongs.

3. Make two small holes through the back of the card,
   at the bottom, and thread a prong through each
   hole. Fix the top of the wire (the loop) to the
   back of the card with washi tape. Angle the wire
   prongs upwards to become your candle holders.

4. Paint a brown frame around your mirror.

5. Once the paint is dry, thread your wire prongs
   with beads, top with a sequin and secure with
   hot-melt glue (leave a little wire at the end for
   your candle).

6. Coat each candle section with thick white
   acrylic paint. Leave to dry, then paint orange
   and red flames on the tips.

{ This can also
be made with
a picture in
place of foil }

PARLOUR GAMES
A PLENTY

The parlour is a
room for receiving
guests and Violet,
as we know, loves to
entertain. It's the
perfect place to
sip tea, discuss the
weather and talk love,
life and friendship.
With bonnet poised,
Miss Violet awaits
your arrival.
So don't be late!

Love Letters

STRAIGHT FROM
VI'S HEART

- paper
- scissors
- ink pen
- violet ink
  (scented optional)
- glue stick

LOVE LETTERS

'I memorize every line,
 I kiss the name that you sign,
 And darling, then I read again right from the start,
 Love letters straight from your heart.'

[From 'Love Letters' by Edward Heyman]

Rarely has a lady been quite so loved as
our Miss Vi, and a pile of love letters
are delivered thrice daily to her door.
Violet has a kind heart, so will sweetly
reply *Return to Sender*, using her special
violet-scented ink.

To feel in demand or simply write the
old-fashioned way, use a pen with special
violet ink. Scented ink is, of course,
optional, and will add a little *je ne
sais quoi* to your mail.

1. Cut a length of paper approximately
   5cm/2in x 2.5cm/1in.

2. Fold the paper into three and snip the
   corners off at one end (as pictured on
   page 86).

3. On the middle section, write a little
   wish for yourself or someone special.

4. Fold the paper to make an envelope
   (as pictured) and glue the top down
   lightly.

5. Seal with a loving kiss (S.W.A.L.K.) or
   a violet heart (optional).

LONDON'S BURNING
LONDON'S BURNING
FETCH THE ENGINE
FIRE! FIRE!

Fire! Fire!

COME ON BABY, LIGHT MY FIRE

- card
- scissors
- glue stick
- acrylic paint (brown, black,
  red, orange, yellow, white;
  gold optional)
- paint brush
- flickering flame battery
  tea light (optional)

FIRE! FIRE!

There really is no place cosier than
a chair by the fire on a chilly eve.
It's also a terribly handy place for
Vi to toast her crumpets, rosy her
cheeks and keep her toes warm.
A well-earned break for our Vi - sweet
dreams by the flickering flames.

1. Cut a piece of card as a base for your
   pieces (here I have cut a 7.5cm/3in x
   7.5cm/3in square).

2. Take some more card and cut out two
   pieces measuring 7.5cm/3in x 2.5cm/1in
   for the columns, a 7.5cm/3in x 2.5cm/1in
   piece for the mantle and four 2.5cm/1in
   squares for decoration on the corners
   of the columns.

3. Glue all the pieces of card into
   place on the base card, leaving the
   inside of the fire empty.

4. Paint the surround brown, then paint the
   inside of the fire place black and leave
   to dry.

5. Paint extra decorative details on the
   columns, corners and mantle as you wish.
   Finally paint the flames of the fire red,
   orange and yellow, with flicks of white.
   (Alternatively, you can cut out the centre
   of the fireplace and use a flickering flame
   battery tea light to add a warming glow to
   the parlour.)

'Tis the Season to be Jolly
TWINKLE TWINKLE LITTLE STAR

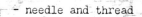

- needle and thread
- sequin stars
- scissors
- beads (7mm or 8mm)
- washi tape (optional)

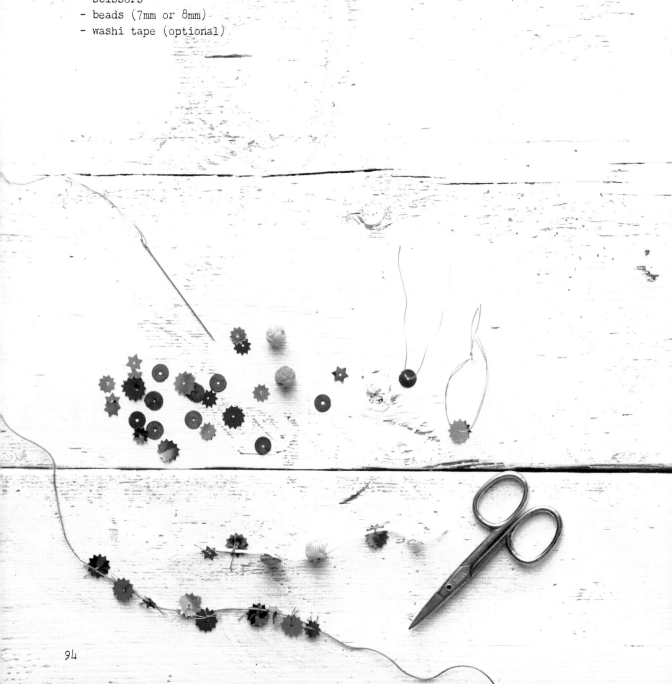

OH, CHRISTMAS TREE

- pine cone or fir cone
- acrylic paint (green)
- paint brush
- glitter
- doll's house tinsel or
  a pipe cleaner
- beads (8mm)

- sequin stars
- angel scrap (see page 169)
- hot-melt glue gun
- plumbing olive/washer or
  a bottle cap/lid (for a
  tree stand)
- scissors

'TIS THE SEASON TO BE JOLLY

'Twas the night before Christmas, when all thro' the house
Not a creature was stirring, not even a mouse;
The stockings were hung by the chimney with care,
In hopes that St. Nicholas soon would be there.'

[From 'A Visit from St. Nicholas' by Clement Clarke Moore]

Are there mince pies for Father Christmas and carrots for
his reindeer? Then away to your manger, Miss Violet,
and rest your weary head.

CHRISTMAS GARLAND

1. To make a star garland, simply
   thread a sequin star on to a
   5cm/2in length of cotton. Sew a
   loop in the centre of the sequin.
   Secure in place with a knot and
   trim as required.

2. Repeat with more sequins and cotton
   threads. When you have enough stars,
   cut some more thread - I used a
   30cm/12in piece but it can be as
   long or short as you wish. Thread
   all your sparkly stars (so that
   the stars will face forward on your
   garland) and some beads, if you'd
   like, along the thread. Secure each
   item in place with a knot as you work.

3. Trim any excess thread away from the
   stars and then tie up your garland,
   or attach it to the corners of
   your room with some small pieces
   of washi tape.

CHRISTMAS TREE

1. To make a Christmas tree, first cover
   your cone with green paint.

2. Sprinkle some glitter over the cone
   before it has completely dried.

3. Once the paint is dry, thread some
   tinsel around your tree.

4. Glue some bead baubles and sequin stars
   onto the edges.

5. Secure your angel scrap on top of the
   tree with glue.

6. Place your tree on to the washer/olive
   or bottle cap/lid tree stand.

MISS VIOLET'S CHRISTMAS

{ Are you hanging up your stocking on the wall? }

BOUDOIR AND EN SUITE

A Place Where Dreams are Made

The bedroom, or boudoir, can be the cosiest
place on earth - a secret place for relaxation
with late-night films, sweet dreams, cold cream,
pampering and nail varnish, and Violet's favourite
- a jolly good book.

An en-suite is an added bonus for sweetly scented
baths and fragrant aromas; whilst not imperative,
one does love a pink sink.

And so 'To bed! To bed!' Said Sleepy-head.

Pressed Flower Wallpaper

GIVE YOUR WALLS A NEW LEAF OF LIFE

- flowers (here I have used a selection from the
  garden including daises, ragged robin, angelica,
  cornflowers and leaves)
- flower press or heavy book
- scissors
- paper till roll or thin strips of paper
  (enough to fit the dimensions of your walls)
- water-based glue
- paint brush
- glue stick (for hanging your wallpaper)

PRESSED FLOWER WALLPAPER

One of the most useful items from my childhood was a flower
press. Simply press and store flowers from any season and use
them as needed. Don't worry if you don't have an actual flower
press - you can always use a heavy book instead. When it comes to
wallpaper, Miss Violet is of course extremely partial to violets -
in white, blue and mauve.

1. Choose and press your flowers; leave in the
   press or heavy book for 1 week.

2. Cut a piece of till roll or paper strip to
   your desired length, and paint a thin layer
   of water-based glue over the top.

3. Arrange your flowers in a pattern across the
   paper (as pictured) and leave to dry.

4. Once the glue is dry, paint a second layer of
   glue over the top of the flowers to seal.

5. Once the wallpaper is completely dry, turn
   it over and roll a glue stick over the back.

6. Hang the paper in your room, starting from
   the top and smoothing down to the end.

you're my wonderwall

The Nights are Drawing In

IT'S CURTAINS FOR YOU

- tape measure or ruler
- fabric or lace of choice
- scissors
- needle and thread
- ball-head pins

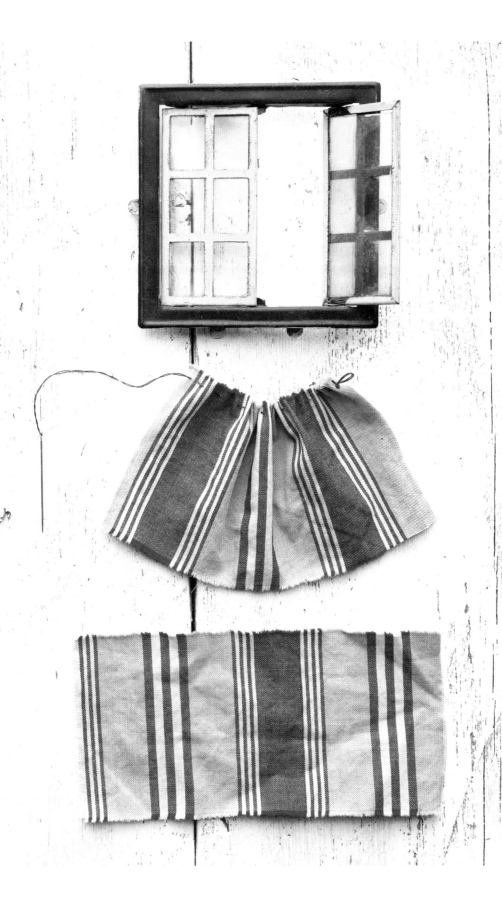

THE NIGHTS ARE DRAWING IN

One of the most important things about a bedroom is getting the light just right. Whether you like a very dark room or one with filtered light, you will need curtains for modesty's sake, if nothing else.

This is such a simple make, so why not add a little more 'boudoir' with a lace curtain too? This method can also be used to make room dividers for an en suite or door. Frippery fancies.

Here I have made very simple curtains from a scrap of old ticking I had in my sewing bag. Of course, yours can be opulent, satin, velvety, trimmed and beribboned, tasselled and lacy, pom-pommed and gilded...

There are a few ways to make a window; you may of course already have one in an existing doll's house, but if using a box, a paper cut-out one will do.

1. Measure your window and decide on the length of your curtains; be sure to double the width of the whole window, as you will be gathering the fabric.

2. Once you have your measurements, cut out a rectangle of fabric, then cut it in half for the curtains to become a pair. Hemming is optional.

{ This method can also be used to make room dividers }

3. Using a needle and plenty of thread, first make a knot and then a tiny loop at one end of a curtain (as pictured on the previous page). Next, sew a running stitch along the top pelmet of both curtains.

4. Hold against your window to check the gathering is the perfect shape, then make another knot and tiny loop at the end of the other curtain.

5. To hang your curtains, use a ball-head pin to fasten one loop to the top of one side of the window, and repeat on the other side.

BATH TIME

Showers are à *la mode* but
Violet has always loved
bubbles - and what better way
to relax than a long soak in
the bath with her favourite
scented bath crème? Warm
dry towels, sprinkled rose
petals, classical music,
dreams of being a mermaid...

Magic Carpets

UP, UP AND AWAY
(ON MY BEAUTIFUL RUG)

- embroidery thread in several colours
- embroidery needle
- playing cards
- ruler
- scissors

MAGIC CARPETS

A beautiful rug is *de rigueur* for crinkled bath
toes everywhere.

Vintage playing cards can be found at markets, thrift stores
or online auctions and often have rather beautiful images.
Here I have used a 1950's card with a sweet deer; I also love
the sides with suits, so don't worry if you can't find pretty
ones - standard playing cards work just as well. These rugs are
versatile and can be made for any room, in any size.

1. Thread your needle with 10cm/4in of embroidery thread and
   make a knot at the end.

2. Push the needle into the card, and then sew again
   (through the same hole) to create a loop of thread around
   the edge of the card (as pictured on page 114). Knot to
   secure, leaving a tail of embroidery thread in place.

3. Trim the thread to make your first fringe tuft. Repeat
   until you have hemmed the edges of the card.

Top Drawers

TIDY-UP TIME

- selection of plain or branded matchboxes
- hot-melt glue gun (to stick the matchboxes together)
- ruler
- piece/scrap of fabric (enough to cover the height and width of the matchboxes once stacked, and to decorate the front of the drawers)
- scissors
- glue stick (to attach fabric to the matchboxes)
- map pins

TOP DRAWERS

Drawers are very useful. Miss Violet keeps all manner
of things in them. Drawers within her drawers in fact.
Sometimes those drawers are not very tidy, but we
won't hold that against her. I would like to believe
she has a handsome supply of violet soap in one
drawer, fluffy powder puffs in another and freshly
starched towels in a third, but I think it unlikely.

Many craft companies make plain matchboxes without the
strikers or labelling, but you can use real matchboxes
if you like.

1. Glue three matchboxes on top of each other
   using the hot-melt glue gun and make sure
   the 'drawers' open the right way up. (At
   this point you could also make a tallboy
   by gluing lots of boxes together.)

2. Using a ruler, measure your chest of
   drawers, then take your fabric and cut
   enough so that it fits all the way around
   the chest. Use the glue stick to fix the
   fabric in place and trim to fit.

3. Add some small offcuts of fabric to cover
   the front of your drawers and fix in place
   with the glue stick.

4. For feet, turn the chest of drawers upside-
   down and push a map pin into each corner.

5. To make handles, carefully dab a little
   glue from the hot-melt glue gun onto the
   sharp end of a map pin, then push the pin
   through the centre of a drawer to secure
   the handle. Repeat as necessary.

Fairytale dreaming

The miller's daughter spun straw into gold

Bedtime rituals are such an important part of the day - it's
a time to relax, recover and dream. 'Time for bed', says
Sleepy-head, and Miss Violet is fair worn out. So, with a
hot water bottle and a good book, Vi's off to the land of
nod, to dream of a girl who could spin straw into gold...

Mouse.

Golden Slumbers

SWEETEST DREAMS

- bed
- tape measure
- fabrics of your choice (measure
  your bed before you begin)
- scissors
- needle and thread
- kitchen roll or blanket wool, folded
- pencil
- green glass, pea-shaped bead
  (optional)

GOLDEN SLUMBERS

Once upon a time Miss Violet said, 'Please can you help
me make a comfy bed?'. 'Certainly, dear Miss Vi', said I.

And so I did. For a fairytale feel, choose plenty of
different fabrics and simply pile them high. But one
doesn't need to be a princess to justify lots of mattresses
- I just couldn't resist making more. For the finishing
touch, I have used a simple glass bead for a pea.

1. Measure your bed to get the length and width
   measurements of your mattress, then add an
   extra 2.5cm/1in to each measurement to allow
   for the hem and filling.

2. Once you have taken your measurements, mark
   out two rectangles of fabric. Cut them out and
   lay one rectangle on top of the other
   (right-sides facing).

3. Sew three sides of the fabric together
   (as pictured on the previous page) to create
   a pocket. Turn the pocket inside out.

4. Fold a piece of kitchen roll or blanket wool
   to make four layers and cut the folded roll
   or wool to fit your pocket, then place the
   filling inside.

{ This make can
  also be scaled
  down to make
  pillows }

5. Fold in the unsewn edges of your fabric and
   secure the filling inside with a running stitch.

6. Pile your mattresses high and add a pea.

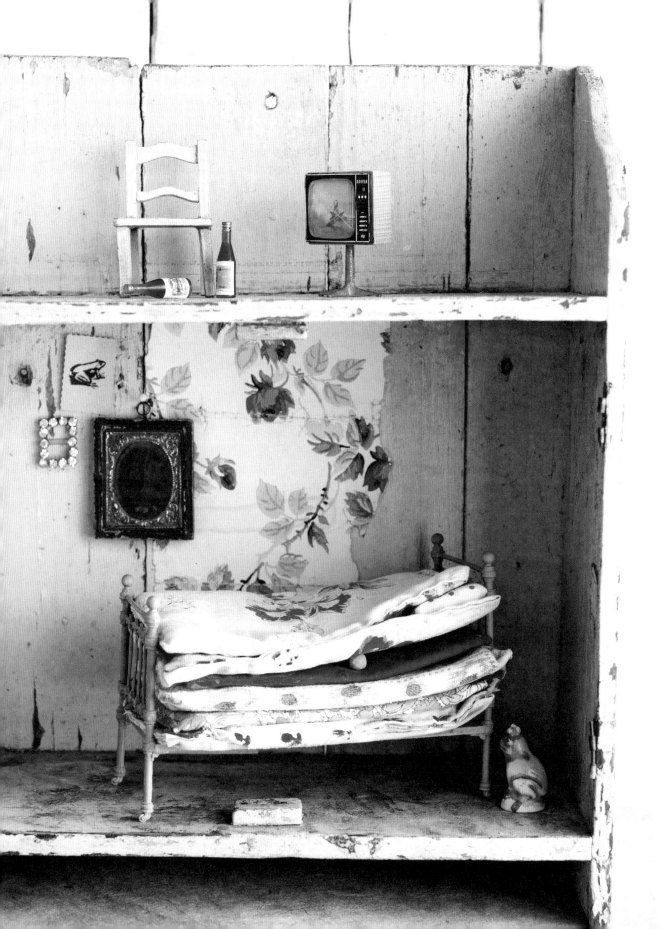

SWEET DREAMS
MISS VI

Far, far away in the
land of fast asleep,
lies Miss Violet
dreaming

GARDEN

Come into the Garden

'Some old fashioned things like fresh
air and sunshine are hard to beat.'

[Laura Ingalls Wilder]

Miss Violet and I adore gardens. We don't necessarily
have green fingers, just rather muddy ones. The joys
of miniature gardening means a single flower stem
becomes a showstopper, a twig becomes a hundred-year-old
apple tree and a tiny compact mirror transforms into
a glistening pond.

Nurturing seeds and plants is hugely satisfying and
some are terribly easy to grow. Why not plant a cress
hedge (also very useful for sandwiches)? Nasturtiums
are wonderful, too, and will make a trail of colour in
only a week or so.

Wait a Minute Mr Postman

LOVE LETTERS STRAIGHT TO YOUR HEART

- plain matchbox
- scissors
- acrylic paint (I've painted mine red with
  black details, but you can choose any mix
  of colours)
- paint brush
- scrap of white paper (you'll need a square
  piece about 2.5cm/1in x 2.5cm/1in)
- glue stick
- postman (optional)

WAIT A MINUTE MR POSTMAN

Miss Violet receives a lot of letters - rather more
than she sends. Some send best wishes, but there are
many declarations of love and admiration, *bien sûr*.

Miss Violet's letters are handled by the postman who
uses a big blue van to transport them straight to her
door without delay.

1. First remove the drawer from the matchbox.
   Next, cut a small slit into the outer part
   of the matchbox through which your letters
   can be posted.

2. Now paint your matchbox and the end of the
   drawer red and leave to dry. Return the
   drawer to the box.

3. Cut out a small square from your paper scrap
   and glue onto the front of the box.

4. When dry, paint a thin black border around
   the letter slot, then either paint a
   squiggle or write your collection times
   neatly on your letterbox. Leave to dry.

5. To collect your letters each day, simply
   pull the drawer out of the box.

Clothes Line

BLOWING IN THE BREEZE

- thin braid or string 30cm/12in long
- scissors
- 2 small branches or twigs,
  approximately 13cm/5in long, or tall
  seasonal flowers (such as lupins,
  sunflowers or delphiniums)
- modelling clay or poster tack
- paperclips of various colours or
  tiny pegs

CLOTHES LINE

Does anything smell quite as nice
as line-dried washing - clothes
infused with fresh air and
sunshine? Or so they say. (Gin and
tonic and chips spring to mind...)

Don't air your dirty laundry,
as the saying goes, but in Miss
Violet's case, her dresses are
just so divine, she is proud to
show them off.

1. Cut some braid or string to your required length.

2. Secure two small branches or twigs to the base of
   your garden with modelling clay or poster tack.

3. Tie each end of your washing line to the branches.

4. Hang up your washing with colourful paperclips or
   miniature pegs.

LAUNDRY DAY IS
A FAMILY AFFAIR

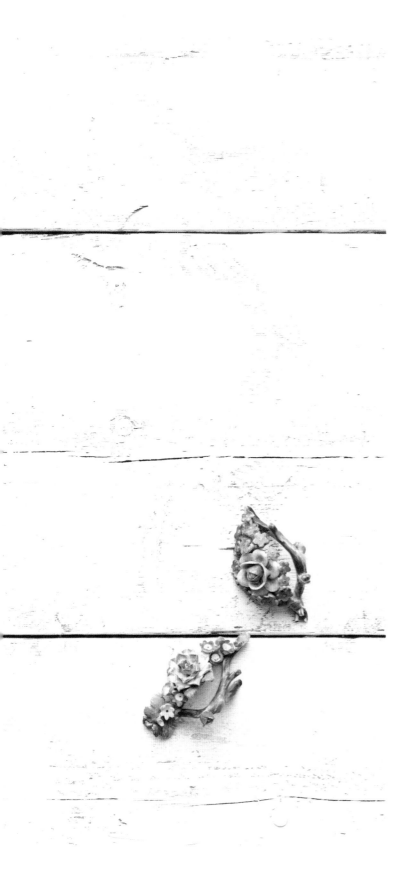

Garden Pond

BLUE LAGOONS AT THE BOTTOM
OF THE GARDEN

- small mirror
- soil
- twigs
- seasonal flowers
- frog (optional)
- swans or ducks (optional)
- panda and rabbits (optional)

GARDEN POND

I like to think there is a little bit of
wishing well, just that tiny bit of magic,
in every pond. That little urge to throw
in a coin and make a wish... Well there's
certainly a little bit of magic in Violet's
pond, and Charming - a prince amongst frogs
- is hoping to catch her eye.

1. Find the perfect spot in your garden.

2. Place your mirror flat on the garden floor.

3. Sprinkle a little soil carefully around
   your mirror.

4. Arrange your twigs and flowers in the soil.

5. Place your frog prince on the mirror
   (he's so vain).

Instant Garden

HOW DOES YOUR GARDEN GROW?

- scraps or pictures of plants and flowers
  (see pages 166-185)
- scissors
- cocktail sticks
- washi tape
- poster tack or modelling clay
- thimbles

INSTANT GARDEN

Violet and I adore this make as it is so very versatile.
Fill your garden with flowers and plants - you can
always use real leaves and flowers here instead of
scraps. Sprinkle some soil in your garden to make
miniature flowerbeds as these upside-down thimbles
become perfect mini plant pots.

1. Choose some scraps or pictures of plants
   and flowers (or draw your own).

2. Cut out and trim as required.

3. Take a cocktail stick and washi tape
   the scrap onto the stick (as pictured on
   page 148).

4. Take a little poster tack or modelling
   clay and roll into a ball; place inside
   the bottom of a thimble.

5. Push the cocktail stick into the poster
   tack or clay.

6. To help your thimble stand up, roll a
   tiny piece of poster tack and secure the
   thimble on top in position.

Strawberries and Dreams

STRAWBERRY FIELDS

- piece of red fabric cut into a circle of
  7.5cm/3in diameter (or go bigger if you wish)
- scissors
- red thread
- household needle
- cotton wool
- green embroidery thread
- embroidery needle

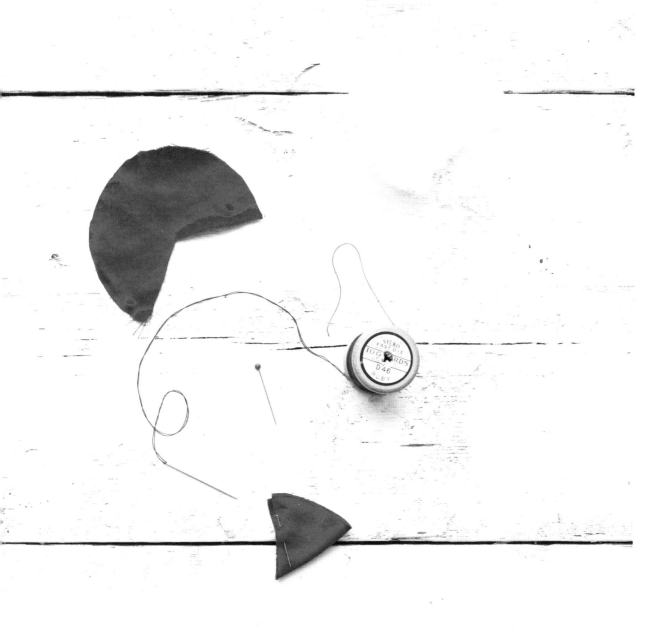

STRAWBERRIES AND DREAMS

Be sure to get your 5-a-day and enjoy the taste
explosion of a giant fruit. Find the juiciest, most
succulent, scarlet strawberry, collect your supper
in a wheelbarrow, and then tuck in.

1. Take your circle of red fabric - here I have
   used a circle with a diameter of 7.5cm/3in.

2. Now cut out a one-third portion (as pictured
   on page 153).

3. Fold the cut portion in half (right-sides
   together) to form a rough triangle shape.

4. With your red thread and sewing needle, sew
   the edges together lengthways (as pictured on the
   previous page) with a running stitch.

5. Turn inside out so you have an ice cream
   cone shape.

6. Fill with cotton wool.

7. With your red thread and sewing needle, sew
   a running stitch around the top and pull taut to
   enclose the cotton wool.

8. With your green thread and embroidery needle,
   sew a green stalk and star shape on the top of
   your strawberry.

Magic Star Garland
STARRY, STARRY NIGHT

- scissors
- thread
- star stickers
- glue stick
- poster tack or modelling clay
- 2 twigs with lots of mini branches

MAGIC STAR GARLAND

'Star light, star bright, first star I see tonight,
I wish I may, I wish I might, have the wish I wish tonight.'

[From 'Star light, Star bright']

This star garland is really simple to make and creates the perfect lighting for a magical midnight feast. (It's also terribly useful for wrapping gifts.)

1. Cut a length of thread (I used 25cm/10in).

2. Stick stars centrally onto the thread using a glue stick.

3. Turn the thread and stars over.

4. Stick another star onto the underside of each star on the thread and press firmly together.

5. Secure one of your twigs to the floor with poster tack or clay and tie one end of the garland to a branch.

6. Repeat with the second twig and secure the other end of your garland. Enjoy a starlit night.

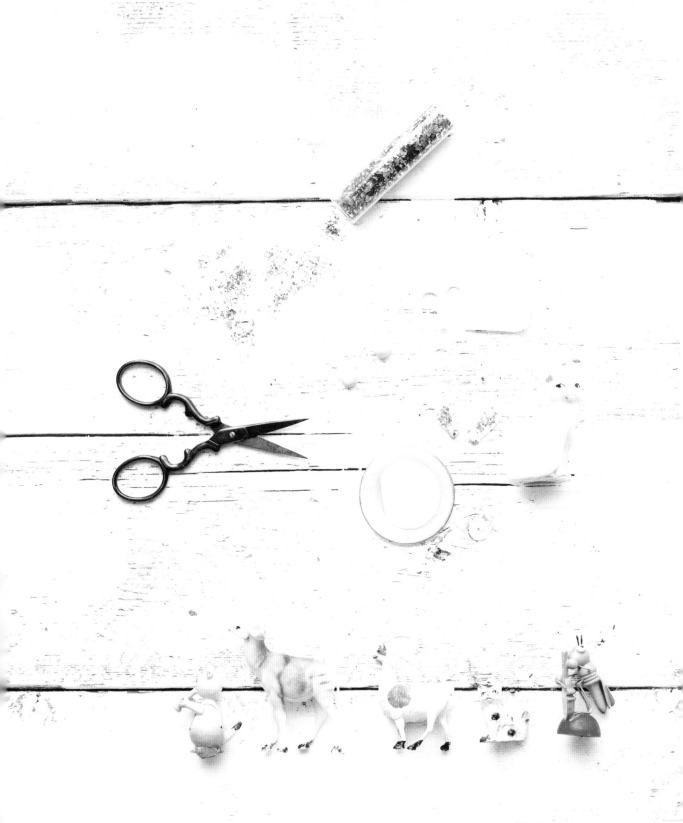

Beautiful Creatures

Roll up, roll up!
Get your wings here!

- selection of miniature creatures
- paper
- scissors
- water-based glue or glue stick
- glitter
- poster tack

BEAUTIFUL CREATURES

Obviously all creatures are a little bit magical but to give Miss Violet's creatures that *je ne sais quoi*, just add wings. These are simple to make and very useful as adornments at soirées. Everyone wants to be a fairy.

1. Line up your creatures (no pushing or shoving).

2. Cut out some paper wings; here I have used a simple petal shape for each wing (as pictured on page 160).

3. Put a little glue on the wings, sprinkle with glitter (as pictured on page 160) and leave to dry.

4. Once dry, fix each wing onto your creature with a tiny piece of poster tack and let the magic begin.

MISS VIOLET'S MIDSUMMER'S EVE

It doesn't have to be Midsummer's Eve
to be a magical night, so hang the
garlands, turn on the fairy lights,
empty the pantry, strike up the
band and dance beneath the stars.

We are family.

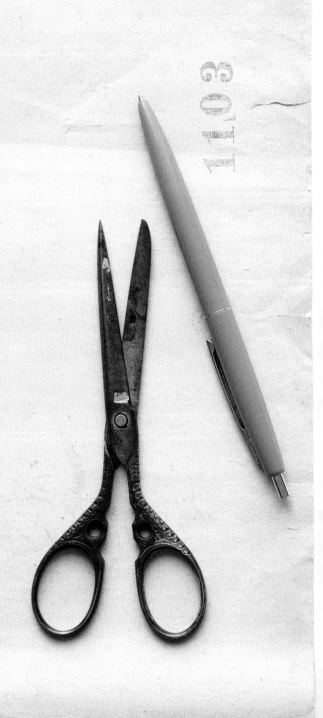

FRISE ASSORTIE

1103

MISS
VIOLET'S
GUIDE
TO
STYLISH
LIVING

La Vie of Miss Vi

Oh my! Violet and I are so excited for you as now we have reached the inspiration pages. Miss Violet, as we know, is terribly chic and on the following pages, you too can achieve a little of this special magic.

I have gathered special antique scraps and drawings of pots and pans, rugs, family portraits and more especially for your doll's house. Photocopy the pages you need, or go to www.pavilionbooks.com/missviolet to download and print.

- kitchen 168

- Christmas 169

- parlour 170

- boudoir and bedroom 171

- *les fleurs* (flowers for walls and floors) 172

- Valentines and violets 173

- friends and creatures 174

- house signs and flowers 175

- Rose Red's perfect looking glass 176

- fabrics for walls and floors 177-183

- roses and cats 184

HOUSE SIGNS AND FLOWERS

Rose Red's
perfect looking glass

RESOURCES

Violet and I like to shop locally and smallest for
us, naturally, is best. You will usually find us at
markets very early in the morning.

Local art shops, charity shops, haberdasheries,
and antiques shops and fairs will offer a wealth
of treasure for finding gems for your doll's
house - and some extra friends for Miss Violet.

Some of my favourite markets...

UK
PORTOBELLO ROAD - Fridays (starts early).
The market runs from the 'flyover'
running northward along Portobello Road,
and then turning right along Golborne
Road, along the right-hand side until
you reach the Lisboa Patisserie where,
if you like, you may reward yourself
with a *pastel de nata* (custard tart) and
a strong coffee.
www.portobelloroad.co.uk

ARDINGLY ANTIQUES & COLLECTORS FAIR -
Ardingly antiques fair in the summer is
bliss. It's so exciting I cannot sleep
the night before.
www.iacf.co.uk

TOTNES MARKET - Quirky combination
market of bread, cottage garden cut
flowers, olives, Indian pyjamas and
lots and lots of junk.
www.totnesmarket.co.uk

USA
BROOKLYN FLEA
www.brooklynflea.com

BRIMFIELD ANTIQUE FLEA MARKETS
www.brimfieldantiquefleamarket.com

AUSTRALIA
CAMBERWELL SUNDAY MARKET
www.camberwellsundaymarket.org

WAVERLEY ANTIQUE BAZAAR
www.waverleyantiquebazaar.com

FRYERSTOWN ANTIQUE FAIR
www.faf.net.au

THE AMAZING MILL MARKETS
www.millmarkets.com.au

PADDINGTON MARKETS
www.paddingtonmarkets.com.au

Social media

INSTAGRAM

I am on Instagram as 'themagpieandthewardrobe'. Please
follow me and say hello. A few of my favourite Instagrammers
include 'galabeerandthedog_vintage', 'seaangels_vintage',
'bodkincreates', 'sidmouth_poppy', 'thewasherwoman' and
'niki_fretwell'. Many Instagrammers also trade doll's
house miniatures.

Useful websites

ETSY AND EBAY
These are both online auction sites, perfect for vintage.
www.etsy.com and www.ebay.com

GREEN & STONE OF CHELSEA
Wonderful art shop in old Chelsea, London, selling
paints, clay, glue, glitter etc.
www.greenandstone.com

BAKER ROSS
Plain white matchboxes and craft supplies.
www.bakerross.co.uk

J. HERBIN
Makers of the fabulous '*Violette Pensée*' ink (violet-scented ink
for writing love letters and bills).
www.jherbin.com

DESIGNERS GUILD
Perfect for fabrics and wonderful velvets. All-round loveliness.
www.designersguild.com

Thank You

Especially and always thank you to my
family: Steve, my love; my beautiful
daughters, Daisy and Ruby; and my
mum. Home is where my heart is.

SPECIAL THANKS

Clare Conville, my agent, who believes in me.

Pavilion, my publishers. Thanks to Polly, David,
Katie, Heather, Claire and Sarah, but most
especially to my editor, Krissy Mallett, a true
believer in Miss Violet, a friend and a jolly
good egg. Also Laura Russell, my art director,
who makes me laugh, leads me from clutter and
helps me make beautiful pages.

Thanks to Tony Briscoe, our photographer,
and Doug Lee, his assistant, who were dragged
into a doll's house book with huge grace and
humour, skill and perfection. The days we spend
at the photo shoots are the best.

Huge thanks to Robin Farquhar-Thomson for my
fabulous author portrait.

Thank you to all of my friends and family who
have helped me whilst writing this book by being
so tolerant of my constant doll's house chatter.

Miss Violet

Miss Violet is a
doll in every way.
She loves...

Very strong coffee
Bedlington lurchers
Albertine roses
Charity shops
Japan
Friends
Old textiles
Northern Soul
Georgian houses
Cream teas
Nick Cave
Markets
Stationery
A real log fire
Incense
Beaches
Festoon lights
Disco and gin.

So does Sam.

Sam McKechnie

Artist, doll-maker, writer, mum. Sam created
The Magpie and the Wardrobe in 2002 as an
extension of her artwork, which is primarily
influenced by folklore and fairy tales.

Sam's collections are sold worldwide through
her stockists in London and Japan and can be
found on Instagram, Facebook and Pinterest
under The Magpie and the Wardrobe, or via her
website www.magpieandthewardrobe.com

She exhibits her artwork every few years.
Information can be found on her social media
pages or via her website.

Sam is the co-author of The Magpie and the
Wardrobe: A Curiosity of Folklore, Magic
and Spells, published by Pavilion.

First published in the United Kingdom in 2017 by
Pavilion
43 Great Ormond Street
London
WC1N 3HZ

ISBN 978-1-911216-13-1

A CIP catalogue record for this book is available from the
British Library.

10 9 8 7 6 5 4 3 2 1

Reproduction by Mission Productions Ltd, Hong Kong
Printed and bound by 1010 Printing International Ltd, China

This book can be ordered direct from the publisher at
www.pavilionbooks.com